EDITORS LETTER

Dear Readers,

Welcome to the first issue of what we hope to be many of 'The Sprocker Spaniel'.

The ethos behind the magazine is to champion and enjoy our beloved Sprockers, not to increase sales of the breed but to revel in our love and enjoyment, dip our toes in new ideas, share experiences and maybe learn something new along the way.

The magazine is for you, so all ideas and feedback and even potential new contributors will be welcomed by all involved.

We are lucky enough to have the support of Lynda Elliott and her hugely successful campaign to 'Recognise the Sprocker Spaniel'. Lynda will be keeping us updated in every issue of her cause and letting us be informed of how 'Sprocker Assit and Rescue' are getting on.

For the time being we are keeping the magazine advert free however if you interested in advertising with us please let us know.

I hope you enjoy the magazine!
ANNE-MARIE MILLARD

CONTENTS

Once upon a time...

It seems important for our first issue to look at where we stand in our lovely Sprocker world. There are lots of differing opinions on the breed (and not all of them good) but maybe now is the time to have a look at the broader picture and decide where we personally want to be whilst understanding other peoples need to move forwards.

However we, as owners, know how brilliant, life affirming and loving a Sprocker can be and that is probably the most important message we can share.

The first point in all of the discussions seems to be that Sprocker are a cross breed when they are simply <u>not</u>. As we will see later on the Sprockers are actually the true forefather of both Cockers and Springers.

At this moment in time the Kennel Club has nine distinct Spaniel breeds recognized by them in total. The Sprocker is not one of them. The result of this is that Sprockers cannot compete alongside their fellow Spaniels and to lots of people this makes a complete mockery of the history of Spaniels.

The Sprocker itself is gaining in popularity, from once being a well-guarded secret of the gundog set – it is now a popular family pet or a 'foot in both worlds' dog for example being a pet by the summer months and a shooting dog come the 'season'. They, as a breed, are very versatile in this respect as long as you choose wisely in the choice of your puppy's parent. As with any spaniel the key to the pups personality takes directly after the parents the majority of the time – so a laid back Springer bitch combined with a gentle Cocker will give you a great family pet. A roaring and ready to go Mother, combined with a focused Father will give you that great working dog.

In fact the general feeling is that the Sprocker owes its more recent roots to a gamekeeper(s) in Scotland who crossed the breeds (Springer x Cocker) to create a dual purpose working dog, combining the best traits of the Springer with those of the Cocker

Richard Bowson, a retired gamekeeper of several decades who now breeds his own Sprockers in North Yorkshire says. 'My local shoot has at least one Sprocker picking up, we don't think to ask each other what our Spaniels actually are, a good dog is a good dog. My Sprocker bitch is as sharp as any Springer or Cocker; she can work a day's shoot and still have energy and enthusiasm for the next day.'

'She was probably one of the quickest of dogs to ever be trained and I have worked with a few over the decades. I am increasingly being asked to produce working Sprocker pups for people, some of the people are new to the Sprocker as a gundog, and others have known their ability for years'.

So what is the problem? There is not just a few (more than 4000 given an estimate) of Sprocker owners who would like the breed to be recognized by the Kennel Club. So far, despite petitions and a fight for their cause, the Kennel Club has stood firm in not recognizing the Sprocker as a breed in its own right. Both experienced gundog owners and the novices can see the Sprocker as being able to do as well as any of the pedigree 'recognized' Spaniels in competing in Working Gundog Trials under the title AV (any variety) Spaniel and do not see why this is not the case for the Sprocker to be able to compete alongside his own family.

Working Clumber Spaniel Society
Field trial
Lichfield Estate

©Farlap
PHOTOGRAPHY

The first port of call in this struggle is Lynda Elliott who has started the Facebook Group 'Recognize the Sprocker Spaniel' – the aim is to educate the public at large and spread the message of the worthy cause – with people joining day by day the group now has over 4,200 members fighting for this recognition.

Of course not every Sprocker owner wants to take part in working trials with their dogs, I would hazard a guess that a lot don't even know what a working trial is. However it is the principle of the thing that the RTSS is asking that at least we should all have the option to if we so desired. On another Facebook group (The Sprocker Spaniel) there was a rather raucous debate when a member suggested he felt the idea of a Sprocker was an 'abomination' of a spaniel – he followed up by saying he could not see why anyone would want to water down the great individual working lines of a Springer and a Cocker. This was followed by a deluge of comments explaining why he was wrong. Whether he left the debate with his tail between his legs (excusing the pun) or with his head held high we will never know.

But with both pedigree Springer and Cocker lines (Cockers particularly) coming from similar lines due to dominant sires there is cause for concern about the lack of genetic diversity. Crossing a Springer with a Cocker will make this problem defunct yet bring a fantastic Spaniel into the world.

At this present moment the Kennel club have not said a blunt 'No' to recognizing the breed either as an AV spaniel or as a type of Spaniel, in fact they have said that they would like to highlight that they do continue to recognize new breeds which is normally done at a request of a breed club. Laura Quickfall from the Kennel Club has said (after the question was put to her regarding recognizing the Sprocker) that they would certainly look into the request of the official breed club on the basis that there are several criteria that the Sprockers must meet. A few of which are more easily met than the others but this is more a subject to be dealt with by itself. Laura said 'Our primary concern is to ensure that all dogs live healthy, happy lives and whilst no formal discussion has started about whether there will begin a more comprehensive register for crossbreeds, we will be asking opinions on whether there is appetite for this amongst breeders and the wider public.'

The sentiment is good; however we are still falling into the category of 'crossbreed'. So where do we go from here? Personal I feel we carry on championing the responsible breeding of Sprockers from registered pedigree lines and carry on the fight to give the Sprocker the recognition it deserves – meanwhile I will go and clean up the muddy paw prints wending their way from the back door to a dog bed containing a snoozing happy Sprocker – what else could you want from life?

A call to arms.......

It all started with a small black puppy, bought from a Gamekeeper at eight weeks old.

I was looking for an English springer spaniel as one of my two had, sadly, passed away and his brother was missing him terribly. I phoned in response to an advert in a local paper and 'Mask' duly became ours. While speaking to his breeder, I enquired about the Sprocker and his reply was 'Aye Lassie, thur takin' the Spaniel back to what they wur before – a real dug!' These wee dugs need to be seen for whit they are...' Twelve years on I can still hear those very words as clear as the light on a summer's day.

Tragically Mask was taken away from us WAY to early at 7 years old in a freak accident. The grief was unbearable – he was, by far, the best Spaniel ever. A fabulous pet that also excelled at going beating with my partner. Our home was empty, it was ghastly.

RAVON

Late one Saturday night we were reading the local paper and there was an advert for Sprocker pups, we phoned, discovered they were 'local' and we were into the car and off. We walked into the most amazing kennel set up ever and here, in front of us, was this pen of eight beautiful Sprocker pups. One just stood out from the rest, as stocky chocolate roan boy with the biggest feet you could imagine. I pointed at him and said 'That one!'

From then Rhum was an integral part of the Elliot-Phillips family and what an addition and adventure that turned out to be.

LYNDA AND JURA

Sitting at work one day – it was lunchtime and I was bored – I decided that Rhum 'needed' his own Facebook page and 'Recognise the Sprocker Spaniel' was born. That was in 2008 – humble beginnings and I remember clearly being ecstatic when I had 50 members on the page!

The ethos has never changed, the passion only grows, that the Sprocker Spaniel should be recognised as AV (Any Variety) Spaniel to enable them to compete alongside the other Spaniel breeds and varieties.

Originally there was one Spaniel – the Land Spaniel. Over a period of time the litters from these Spaniels were categorised according to their height. Those puppies that matured to over

21" at the shoulder were called 'Springing Spaniels' – they sprung the game birds. Those puppies less than 21" were called 'Woodcocking Spaniels' as they went into cover and drove out the smaller birds. Eventually it became the 'norm' to breed all those over 21" together and all those under 21" together thus the Springer Spaniel and Cocker Spaniel became breeds.

So.....let's ask the question – what is a Sprocker Spaniel? It's really not rocket science is it? They are NOT a designer breed: they are NOT a cross breed and they are very defiantly NOT mongrels – they are 100 percent Spaniel.

They are going back to the 'original' Land Spaniel. Unfortunately, as there is no breed standard the Kennel Club will not allow them to compete in any Field Trials or Working Gundog competition they run. When tackled on this subject they absolutely close ranks – the best response was the one we got at Scone Game Fair this year...'it is the way it is' to quote.

But Kennel Club – watch out!! Recognise the Sprocker Spaniel (RTSS) has almost 5000 members and the majority of the membership strive for the same thing – we want our dogs to be recongised as a Spaniel to enable them to compete alongside their pedigreed counterparts on a level playing field. We do not want the Sprocker to be recognised as a breed because the criteria is quite abhorrent!! We just want the KC to admit that when you cross a Springer with a Cocker spaniel the result is 100 % Spaniel!!

The figures speak for themselves – 5000 members on a Facebook page, lots of Sprocker working on shoots – both walked up and driven. Like it or not the Sprocker is here to stay, RTSS is not simply going to go away. The fight will continue, I may not see it myself, but I sincerely hope, one day, I will be granted my desire - one day there will be Sprocker Spaniels competing against the Springers, Cockers, Clumbers and the like. One day they will get their chance to show what a truly magnisficaent variety of Spaniel they are.

They are, after all, the closest thing to a Land Spaniel, ever!

Lynda Elliot
FOUNDER OF RTSS

There is now also Sprocker Assist and Rescue, a 'sister' to RTSS. Established in 2014 , they are the only Sprocker dedicated rescue. Run by a team of avid Sprocker lovers, supported by a fabulous group of volunteers who go above and beyond to assist these dogs, securing them a new loving forever home, regardless of the reason they have ended up with us. Funded entirely by donations and fundraising events SAR is also growing with, so

TO FIND OUT MORE ABOUT 'SPROCKER ASSIT' PLEASE VISIT OUR WEBSITE

www.sprockerassist.org or visit our Facebook pages 'Recognise the Sprocker Spaniel' and 'Sprocker assist and Rescue'

We will be updating news on both Sprocker Assist and RTSS in each edition of this magazine.

FIRST AID

There is probably no time of the year when you don't need a first aid kit for your beloved.....summer months can see sun burn on sensitive noses,winter months bring more rummaging through prickly undergrowth with cuts and tears. We keep our canine first aid kit well out of the way of children since we found all our sticky tape for bandages being used as makeshift masking tape – it now resides in an old grooming box well out of reach. You can purchase lots of ready-made first aid kits in many places (Pets at home, Amazon etc.) but here is a list of essentials:

Emergency numbers – not necessarily the first thing you would think of for a first aid kit, but if you need it in a hurry then its good to have it in a sensible place. A sticky label with the vet's number on, their 'out of hours' emergency number and your microchip number on the inside lid will stand you in good stead.

Bandages – the gauze type bandage so it is non adhesive and doesn't stick to the fur or a wound.

Antiseptic wipes – you can get canine specific ones, but human ones work well too.

'Hibiscub' (surgical scrub/solution) is brilliant to clean out dirty wounds.

Scissors and tape – never there when you need them but obviously important to secure and cut bandages.

Sterile saline wash – good for cleaning out debris out of your dogs eyes.

Sunscreen – use the highest factor sunscreen for babies – this will make it gentle enough for your dog. Do check that it does not contain zinc oxide since this is toxic to dogs. If you can, do a small tester patch on your dog just to make sure he/she is not allergic to it. Pink snouts and the delicate under belly need to be protected from the direct sun.

Thermometer and KY Jelly – If you think your dog has a temperature then its going to need to be a rectal job (they look more surprised than anything else). Normal temperature is 99.5-102.5F.

Ear cleaning solution, worming and flea tablets – always good to have in one place.

Finally a spare lead and muzzle (even the best dogs get grouchy when in an unknown situation, yummy treats always welcome too...

SPROCKETS – THE FIRST TIME SPROCKER OWNERS Q&A

We all never stop learning so what might seem a simple question and answer to one person might be a brand new revelation to another... the main point is to never be afraid to ask. Its this premise that so many of the Facebook dog groups work as such an excellent forum for the complete beginner to the seasoned dog owner. Here we cover some basic problems that you *might* encounter...

> We have recently bought home our new Sprocker puppy who is practically perfect in every way, or she was....she is now jumping up and nipping everybody, though it seems mainly our 8 year old daughter that she likes throwing herself at. Understandably our daughter is now getting very wary of the new addition to the family, which is the last thing we want – what do you suggest?

Let's start with the basics; it's perfectly natural for pups to bite. As they begin to teeth they naturally need things to chew on. Some dogs prefer using their mouths than their paws to move and investigate in this shiny bright new world of theirs (you can think of their mouths being the equivalent of our hands). If you sit and watch a group of young pups playing, it's all about the mouth as they rough and tumble around. When puppies play, they mouth each other, which is totally normal. However when mouthing turns to a bite, the puppy on the receiving end will let out a yelp, and this sound startles the puppy doing the biting, making them release.

We can use this piece of observation to teach our pups to inhibit the bite and learn how much is too much. This is going to require a bit of play acting but it is a very effective way to solve your problem.

When the puppy grabs hold of your hand or finger too hard, let your hand go limp and let out a yelping sound. When the pup releases, ignore her for ten to twenty seconds and then resume playing.

Its important to remember NOT to pull away from the bite. This can trigger your puppys chase instinct and make the problem worse. Don't repeat this process more than three times in fifteen minutes – if you get to that point its time to stop playing and for your pup to have a bit of time out – so put her in her bed/crate area and walk away. So this is teaching the pup that gentle play continues and rough play STOPS.

You can also redirect the pup. When she tries to mouth you, pull your hand away quickly and provide a treat or wave around a chewy toy to she bites that. Good Luck!

Junior Owners Points of View

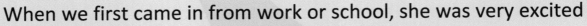

My pup, April, is brilliantly behaved now as we have control, however before when we didn't, things were different. Young pups, like April, have their mad fives and they always will. So don't worry.

When we first came in from work or school, she was very excited to see us. She would jump up and we would try to push her down, with our hands. That to April seemed that we were playing with her, so it made her jump more and nip. This can be caused by high pitched squeals so we tried and lowering the tone and didn't go crazy ourselves, even though she like all spaniels are adorable.

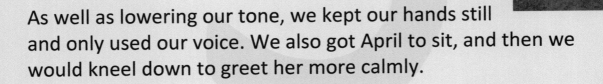

As well as lowering our tone, we kept our hands still and only used our voice. We also got April to sit, and then we would kneel down to greet her more calmly.

Now she has stopped jumping up and certainly stopped nipping at us when we are playing. So she is now the perfect puppy (with help from us of course!).

SAMANTH BARNARD

Its been a long time since I trained my dog to walk to heel and am just about to take possession of a new pup. I have been reading up on various theories and am now more confused than ever! I also have already started worrying about when and how I should let him off the lead and if he will come back....what would you recommend please?

Sally Dixon

Walking to heel

Walking to heel is the most boring exercise you can ask a dog to do, so with pups I tend to just do short training sessions on the lead so you have their attention. However we are the ones that create a 'puller' as we tend to let pups off the lead too early, our intention is good of course, but the result can be counterproductive!

Why would a pup happily walk on a lead if we gave him all the freedom to begin with and, now, we are trying to rope him up on the walks? The pup knows what 'walkies' is about now so he will pull you all the way to the park in hope that once there he will be let off this horrible lead. I normally suggest before you let your pup have all the freedom teach him to walk on the lead nicely. Nice and easy heel work achieved by lots of short training sessions.

Recall

Again we spoil it, not the dog! Every time the pup gets called back to its owner he finds himself leashed up again so the dog learns that if I come back I lose my freedom. The best way to begin is to have something yummy in your pockets and a tennis ball or toy to throw. During every walk just call the pup in to give him a treat and cast the pup away again or throw a toy for him. So each time your pup comes back he learns it can be fun ad it doesn't always mean he will lose his freedom.

Ilona Bush works as a dog, pup and gundog trainer in Norfolk.If you would like to send her a question for another issue please email at:

thesprockerspanielmagazine@gmail.com

There are still (surprisingly) some people that don't actually know what at Sprocker is. However it is not just day to day people like ourselves that realise the greatness of the dog, the police have long known about the exceptional balance the cross between the Springer and the Cocker can bring.

Now retired aged 11, Springo the Sprocker begun duties with dog handler PC Ian Tolchard based at Cambourne in Cambridgshire. Originally adopted from' Plymouths Gables Farm cats and dogs home', Springo trained firstly for drugs searches and then for firearms and cash.

PC Tolchard said 'His record of work is excellent. On one occasion he found a hidden assault rifle which had been used to threaten members of the public. On another successful job he managed to locate large sums of hidden cash which was being smuggled out of the county from local ports.Over in the West Midlands Police force, a litter of six sprockers were born back in August 2014. These three boys and three bitch pups are the forces first Sprocker litter overseen by Dave Raymond who is the breed scheme manager at the dog unit in Balsall Common; He said 'what we are trying to achieve in breeding Sprockers is to bring out certain temperaments in each of the breeds; our Springer Spaniels tend to be a little gamey, meaning they like to chase birds, but the Cockers can be quite responsive so we are hoping we can create the ideal search dog by combining the two.

We have had Sprockers donated to us before and the ones we have got work very well and have a great nose of them.The pups went to homes with puppy walkers who will have looked after them until they are about a year old – puppy walkers are vital to the training school and help orientate dogs for the first 12 months of their lives, allowing them to experience what it is like living in a home, socializing with people and other animals – Dave Raymond says 'after their time with the puppy walker's, they go on an eight week course to develop their search instincts, they will complete searches in buildings, streets, open spaces and vehicles going on to be either a drug sniffer dog or a specialist dog depending on what they show aptitude to for.

Places to visit. eat. drink. stav and love.

Sprockers do like to be beside the seaside.....

This month –Suffolk coastline

Whether you are enjoying the quaint beach huts and old lighthouse in Southwold, or wandering through the historic town of Bury St Edmunds, Suffolk is tucked neatly away in the far eastern part of the UK. Its coastline contains miles of hidden beaches, bordering onto areas of natural beauty such as Minsmere or Dunwich – both great dog walking country. From there you can move inland along winding country roads moving through thatched pink cottages surrounded by wisteria and roses. All of it being a perfect weekend hideaway or a great old fashioned seaside holiday. Crabbing at Walberswick and a good pub lunch is every Sprockers day dream, though many places these days are not too dog friendly. But here are some that are and come highly recommended by the Sprockers themselves.

Southwold – The Harbour Inn

Blackshore by the boats, from A1095, turn right at the Kings Head pub in Southwold and follow road down past the golf course and water tower. IP18 6TA

This is a favorite place of lots of people, with lots of boat and people watching going on too. You can choose to sit outside or tuck yourself in the nautical themed back bar with dark paneling and scrubbed tables. There are lot of locals that use the pub, and lots of visitors too. Big plates of food, bowls of water for the dogs, and cheerful staff. Great place to take a walk along the harbor itself, if you walk inland you will come to the bridge which takes you across into Walberswick. Dogs are allowed in the bar, children welcome away from the top bar. Open 11-11.

www.harbourinnsouthwold.co.uk

Southwold – Lord Nelson

East street, off High Street (A1095) IP18

Affectionally known as the 'Nellie' by the locals, this pub is usually over spilling with laughter, chatting, and smell of good beer and food. There is a partially paneled traditional bar and its two small side rooms are kept immaculately with good lighting and roaring coal fire in the winter months. There are some interesting Nelson memorabilia (hence the name) and a great model of HMS Victory. There are seats out the front with a side view down towards the beach and a sheltered back garden. Children and dogs both welcome. Open 10.30am to 11.00pm. 12.00 to 10.30 on a Sunday.

www.thelordnelsonsouthwold.co.uk

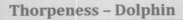

Thorpeness – Dolphin

Thorpness, Leiston, Suffolk IP16 4NB

Neat extended pub with three lovely rooms for guests. Very interesting village to visit with a short walk to the beach itself. With plenty of seats outside the Dolphin also has a Scandinavian feeling to its main bar with pale wooden tables and chairs on a quarry tiled floor.

www.thorpenessdolphin.com

Aldeburgh – Cross Keys

Crabbe Street, Aldeburgh, Suffolk IP15 5BN

Cheerful 16th century pub near the beach (good dog walking place too). The back terrace looks across the promenade to the water. Inside the pub itself you will findwelcoming atmosphere, low ceilinged interconnecting bars with antique and other putype furniture, the landlords collection of oils and Victorian watercolours, painting by local artists and roaring log fires in two inglenook fire places. There are two resident dogs and all dogs welcome in any part of the pub and in the three furnished b&b rooms.

www.aldeburgh-crosskeys.co.uk

St James Street

Once a great port, Dunwich is now a tiny village gradually sinking into the sea. The Ship was once a well-known smugglers inn, almost on the beach overlooking the salt marsh and the sea. It has an old fashioned bar with nautical knick-knacks, flagged floor and simply furnished. There is a modern dining room and up the Victorian staircase you will find some simple, uncluttered bedrooms with period features, cord carpets and brass bedsteads. From here it is a moments' walk to the beach, with long stretching dunes, perfect for dog walkers. On the beach itself (in the car park) is a great fish and chip restaurant, often packed in the height of the season and closed during the winter months.

GUNS 'N GALS

Traditionally shooting is a man's game, they disappeared off for the 'season' calling in the little women to top up hip flasks and provide pork pies and sandwiches at the required moments. Fortunately now, time are changing and more and more women are found gun in hand. With shooting schools seeing the gap in the market and , with the help of social media, all female shooting syndicates growing rapidly, the traditional world of gundogs and shooting is edging its way into change.

But how are the men taking it? We have spoken to women who are helping make the change, whether they are shooting, in the beating line, or picking up: however there are not many who are completely happy to be blunt and truthful for fear of 'upsetting' their fellows on the field.

However Sarah Woodhouse has been talking to us (brave woman!), 'I do have the upper hand to most, my father and generations of his family are local landowners and own the shooting rights to quite a large area where we live. I was brought up with the 'guns', my Father teaching me to shoot from aged ten, '

'I always enjoyed our days out as I was growing up even though it meant I was the one in the back of the land rover holding on to my Fathers filthy Spaniels. I was treated like one of the boys and they rarely curtailed their language or content on my behalf. As I got older it became less interesting until my Father suggested I joined the shoot as one of the 'guns'. I am not sure what the other men made of it, and I was often the butt of most jokes, however since my skill soon over shadowed theirs, I found they soon shut up! These days we have two other women on the shoot, I am surprised they stayed following their first season with us, I did my best to stick up for them but that really did not help in any shape or form. However the 'gal's' just tightened their lips and got on enjoying themselves and not worrying about any of the ribbing they were getting. I think the novelty has now worn off for the men in general so they are left in peace to enjoy their hobby. I certainly would recommend shooting to any women who like the great outdoors in this beautiful country, it is a test of skill and friendship with your dog, it is a great institution.'

So you don't have to actually shoot to enjoy the day out. There are plenty of other jobs to be involved in, if you are not bothered about picking up a shotgun. Amanda Pratt has one seasoned

Sprocker 'Archie' and a new puppy ('Eddie') waiting in the wings; 'I was bought up in the country like Sarah, and have been involved in shooting since I was a child. My late husband was a keen shot and had a gun in a shoot in Norfolk from his mid-twenties until he died at the age of 41. I became much more involved with beating and 'picking up' after I moved to Suffolk after my husband died. I originally had a very unruly Jack Russell terrier however people kept suggesting I got a 'gundog' to work

with since they thought it would be more fun for me. I actually think, in retrospect, they meant a well behaved Labrador but both my late husband and myself had always yearned for a Spaniel. In 2007 I have already chosen a Welsh Springer pup but I got cold feet and put off having him, I was sitting in the beaters lorry early one shooting season and was admiring one of their Springer Spaniels to which he replied, 'she has just had a litter of 11 and there is a lovely tri-coloured dog pup that I think you would like', of course seeing Archie for the first time tottering towards me, I was hooked.

'I really had no idea of what I was taking on and certainly had no idea of how to train a gundog and it took me a little while to realise that I really did need some help! After enrolling in some obedience classes (naughtiest pup ever to grace their floorboards) and trying one to one lessons with a variety of gundog trainers (a lot of time was spent training me more than the dog) I discovered the secret was to find a trainer that was not just good for the dog but for me too and to have one that has a particular interest in Spaniels.

From then on I am now picking up on two shoots on a weekly basis and on a variety of smaller shoots on a Saturday. The only discrimination I have found has been from 'commercial people' (not the regulars) who have suggested to another male' picker up-er' that they should check to make sure I have done the job properly and not missed anything! It is rare though. There are less women than men, and it is still predominantly a man's world, but as long as you carry your sense of humour with you and don't mind being teased it is a great way to meet new and interesting people and get out and aoubt in the otherwise rather bleak English winter.

If shooting itself for whatever reason, ethical or otherwise, does not interest you then maybe Gundog training with your Spaniel is a step in your direction. There are many Gundog trainers out there, a lot of them women, and not your stereotypical Barbara Woodhouse type either! Ilona Bush is one of those and now our resident dog training expert on the magazine.

There are many interesting ways we as women can become more involved in this vibrant world — we just need to know where to start! For more information :- thesprockerspanielmagazine@gmail.com

Tilly's Tasty Treats

Nothing tells your Sprocker that you love them more than a bit of time spent baking something delicious for them. Tilly (and her Mother) have spent a long while perfecting her tasty treat cookbook, with many an eager taste tester sitting below her feet.

Gingerbread dogs
These smell divine to humans and taste delicious to our canine friends.

Ingredients

225grams brown rice flour
1 tsp baking powder
1tsp ginger
1 tsp cinnamon
½ tsp baking soda
1 egg
60ml sunflower oil
120ml molasses
2 heaped tbs of unsalted peanut butter
1 tb. Apple cider vinegar

Apple Cider Vinegar

You can't go wrong with apple cider vinegar even if you are human or canine, it works for you both inside and out...
Introduce it to your dogs water bowl a drip at a time working your way up to a teaspoon a day (have a glug yourself while you are it!).

ACV is good for arthritis, allergies, itchy skin, eliminating tear stains around yor dogs eye and fighting fleas...

Preheat the oven to 180 degrees Centigrade. Combine all the ingredients together and mix thoroughly until a dough forms. Roll the dough out on a lightly floured surface to a cm thickness. Using a cookie cutter cut out all the treats and place on an ungreased baking sheet. They don't tend to spread so they can be quite close together.

Bake 18-22 minutes or until the edges are golden brown. Let them completely cool on a wire rack. Store at room temperature in a loosely covered container.Tie a yellow ribbon...

Tie a yellow ribbon..

If you are born of a certain age then 'tie a yellow ribbon round the ol' Oak tree' will be reminding you of 1970's flares and 'Top of the Pops'. However do you know what it means if you see a yellow ribbon around a dog's collar? It took me a moment of internet searching to find out and, considering I own a shy dog, I am rather ashamed to say I hadn't heard of it before that day.

This gentle symbol is the brainchild of Terry Ryan who established this gentle signal in her canine camps and classes. It was then introduced into Australian Dog Clubs in early 2000 by Pat Robards after asking Terry if she could borrow the idea for her shy dog 'Bo'. Now the idea seems global, spanning the continents to our shores.

As dog owners I feel we should know, understand and educate others in regard of this great idea. It acts as a signal that means this dog needs some space, just like an amber traffic light is a signal to approach with caution. It is to help people (especially kids) identify that this is NOT the dog to be running at, but the dog that needs to be approached slowly and any interaction discussed with the dogs handler before any attempts to pat the dog. It does NOT mean the dog is aggressive in any shape or form. You would not believe the amount of times I have had parents get on a high horse and start judging my Spaniel when I have asked kids not to rush up to her – their initial reaction is that she is going to bite their children and I am an awful person for bringing this dog into humankinds vicinity.

She (Sally the Spaniel) has had a bad experience with the human race and is simply scared of everybody, she is not going to maul your child (or yourselves) and she is trying hard to learn to trust everybody and anybody again. And the other way to do this is to introduce her gradually back into the loud bustling world.

There are lots of reasons why a dog may well use a yellow ribbon. It could be:

- The dog has health issues
- The dog is in training
- The dog is being rehabilitated and learning to socialize (like Sally)
- The dog is scared or reactive around other dogs (like Sally)
- The dog may be ill, hurt, blind, deaf or just old
- They may have a new family and are just getting to know each other
- The dog becomes over excited.

The yellow ribbon works a quick way to communicate the comfort level of a dog avoiding triggering unnecessary panic or stress that can cause unexpected and unpleasant outcomes for everyone involved. It is stressed that this is not an excuse to avoid proper training, not a marker of a dog who has a poor temperament and NOT a responsibility. It is stressed that this programme is not about (or for) aggressive dogs, dogs that bite must wear a muzzle. Does it work? I guess it depends where you are. My experience in Suffolk was that it worked in the quieter months (when the towns around us are quietly busy with local people) but in the tourist season it didn't. The locals, even if they did not know what it meant, stopped in their tracks and asked, giving Sally some space for her to approach them. The tourist season I will avoid forever more – enough said. But it is not just about me...

Nikki and Dave Glasgow live on the Isle Of Wight, their pup Jenson has been shy from the start however they are combatting this by socialising him thoroughly but the key has been having the courage to ask people politely not to rush at him. Slowly but surely they are winning the battle.

I think the lesson for all of us is to adopt the ethos of when people approach our dogs to be able to mention not all dogs are as confident as our own, and all of us to enjoy our dogs, shy, nervous or not. Our dogs are, after all, as diverse as we are!

From our foreign correspondent

My name is Else and I am Danish Sprocker Spaniel. My owner Emilie and I live in a ground floor apartment in Copenhagen. Here is a taste of my delicious Danish life:

6.30am I wake Emilie up by jumping on her bed, this normally wakes up her cat (defiantly NOT my cat) which then in turn also jumps on my owner. This combined effort means we are sitting at the breakfast table by 7.00am.

7.30am we leave for work. Emilie works in a design house and I am the office dog. It is quite long walk to work and we are having many lovely parks in Copenhagen. The park next to my home is called Faelledparken and here I say hello to many of my friends as I pass through. When I was a puppy we used to drive to work or sometimes I would sit in the basket on the back of my owner's bike. Lots of people cycle round the city so it is a great place for cyclists of all ages.

8.15am we arrive at work and I take up residence in my official basket.

11.30am we go out for a walk and for lunch. The office is next to Nyhavn where there are lots of yummy places to eat, interesting places for me to sniff and I get a good walk and a toilet break.

4.30pm we finish work, sometimes we hang round with friends after work and sometimes we just walk back home through the park.

6.00pm we have dinner either in front of the wood burner or out on the terrace depending on the weather. Then bedtime…I fall asleep dreaming of our summers spent up on the coast in the summer house where I can play in the sand dunes, and our winters drifting snow up to my nose. Life cannot be more perfect for an urban Spaniel.

WHISTLE TRAINING FOR BEGINNERS

We all start somewhere; some people are natural sponges with new information whereas others (like me) have to do a lot of frowning, a lot of reading and a lot of asking the same question over and over again. I would like to think that I always get there but some others might disagree! This section is for the people out there like me, eager to learn but don't want to look too silly in front of the general public if

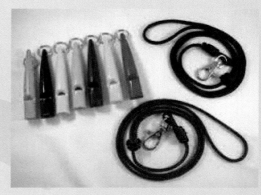

we can help it. This is not meant as highbrow gundog training though it does follow the same premise. I do it because it gives me a lot of satisfaction watching my dog be clever and it gives me a good personal excuse to disappear for some long walks, just me and her.

REASONS FOR USING A WHISTLE

- The sound of a whistle carries further than your voice
- Your kids have given your pup a nickname that is too silly for a grown up to shout.
- A whistle does not convey emotion e.g. frustration, anger, abject desperation....
- A whistle is transferable between handlers ensuring the dog returns to whoever is walking it.

You can start whistle training your puppy from as early as you like. The earlier it is started the quicker is becomes ingrained in them. You do need to appreciate that they are only little so it is best just to do a few minutes here and there, otherwise they will soon become bored and go off in search of mischief...they will soon tell you when they have had enough. A good way to start is to have your whistle around your neck at all times. It needs to be second nature that you put it on first thing (I always put mine on when I brush my teeth), you can then start introducing the whistle when, for example, its food time. A little 'toot toot' to here comes food and a little 'toot' to site. More on this later.

First get organized – buying a whistle is obviously the main thing. These you can buy online, from us, from Amazon, from Ebay and larger pet stores. You will then need your puppies food bowl, the whistle around your neck and your pup.

Get the puppy to sit – most will do this if you hold the food bowl over their head or use the palm of your hand blocking out their line of sight also works

Gently hold the pup still by a gentle restraint either holding the scruff of the neck or the collar.

Put the food bowl on the floor telling your pup to 'leave'.
Get the pup to wait a couple of seconds .

Blow the whistle two short sharp blasts and release the pup allowing them to eat.

DO THIS AT EVERY MEAL TIME FOR AT LEAST A WEEK – YOU WANT THE PUP TO FORM THE WHISTLE/FOOD ASSOCIATION.

You can then start doing this around the house. Have a few dog treats or dog biscuits in your pocket. Have a family member holding the dog within your eyesight. Two short sharp bursts on the whistle, call the pups name, the pup is released and comes running towards you, you reward with a treat and lotsof praise. Everybody happy! Repeat this step MANY times.

use the same two short sharp bursts and lots of praise when the pup finds you. Then you can get more adventurous and start hiding...they will find you eventually....you might need to use the whistle more than once....but sooner or later they will respond to you just giving the call once.

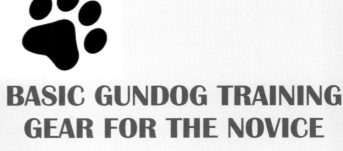

BASIC GUNDOG TRAINING GEAR FOR THE NOVICE

Ok so you have got the dog and the inclination so what do you need to get going on your quest for perfectly trained gundog? You don't need much to 'do it yourself'; you capay a lot of money for one to one lessons (though it is certainly worth it if you find the right person to train you and your dog every now and then) but getting the basic gear does not cost much.

A WHISTLE

This is your first core item, Acme is the one manufacturer that most will recommend. Whistles come in different pitches, we use a 210.5 or, if you prefer an Acme 211.5 which has a lower pitch. There are other 'pitches' but the these are the most commonly used.

Acme whistles used to just be in black but now you can find them in a huge range of colours to suit your mood.

You will also need a lanyard to hang the whistle around your neck. These too come in different colours.

A RETRIEVING DUMMY

A traditional dummy for a young spaniel is a half-pound puppy dummy. You will need two of these.

A SLIPLEAD

A simple gundog slip lead is a standard gundog training issue. They come in various materials and colours. Nylon is usually better than rope since it does not hold moisture and recovers from getting wet at much faster pace.

That's all you need to get started. There is plenty of other equipment you can get spending on at a later date but this lot is all you need for the time being – good luck!

GAME ON!

Pheasant and chorizo paella

As a rural family, breeding gundogs and up and out during the shoot season we make sure we eat the fruit of our labours – namely as much game as we can possibly eat as a family. Sometimes it simple after school suppers (pasta bolognaise with Pheasant as opposed to beef) and sometimes a Saturday cooking session trying out new recipes and consuming some good wines (and occasionally a good consumption of wine). Here is a tried and tested recipe for you to begin with. You don't have to follow the wine selection whilst in the process of cooking but if you do please have a glass for us!

In theory this serves 6 – 8 people or 4 people if you are of a hearty appetite.

Ingredients

1 litre of stock (chicken or pheasant)
¼ tsp saffron strands
3 tbsp. olive oil
8 pieces of pheasant breast
250g spicy sausage cut into chunks
15og chorizo sausage cut into chunks
1 large red onion roughly chopped
4 crushed garlic cloves
400g chopped tomatoes
3 tsp smoked paprika
1 tsp chilli flakes
375g Spanish paella rice
325g jar of roasted peppers
Or
4 home roasted peppers sliced
5 medium eggs
1 tsp chopped flat leaf parsley
Grated zest of ½ unwaxed lemon
Lemon wedges to serve.

Bring the stock to a gentle roll in a saucepan. Stir in the saffron, remove the pan from the heat and set aside.

Pour yourself a glass of pink fizz (our choice is Adnams).

Heat I tbsp. of the oil in a paella pan or wide casserole dish. Seasonthe pheasant on both sides and brown them on both sides (but not cook through). Take the meat out of the pan and set this aside too. Add the sausages and chorizo to the pan and brown them all over. Try and get a few crispy edges for taste and texture. Set   these aside with the meat.

Have another glass of fizz.

Pour off all but 1 ½ tbsp. of fat from the pan. Add the onion and cook until it is soft, gleaming and golden, this takes about four minutes or so, now add the garlic and cook for another two minutes. Add the tomatoes and cook for another four minutes. Stir in the paprika and chilli and cook for a minute, stirring, then add the stock. Return the pheasant, sausage's and chorizo, bring to a simmer and cook over a gentle heat for ten minutes.

By the now the fizz should be exhausted so now we suggest a bottle of Rose d'anjou.

Pour the rice all-round the chicken and season everything to taste. Cook for 25 minutes (set a timer if the wine is going to your head). Don't stir the rice! Preheat the oven to 220 C/425F/gas mark 7.

Ten minutes before the end of cooking time add the peppers tucking them thoroughly in amongst the meat and rice. When the cooking time is up, all the stock should have been absorbed.

Last glass of 'cooking' wine now.

Lightly beat the eggs in a bowl with some salt, pepper, parsley and lemon zest (you can add a fine grating of nutmeg if you have it to hand). Pour the mixture over the top of the paella, tilting the pan from side to side to ensure an even layer of egg. Now put the dish in the over for five minutes. The top should be set and crusty. Serve with your lemon wedges for an added 'zing'.

We have been Sprockered!!!

The Raymond family and their black Sprocker 'Luna'

What is Luna's favorite toy?

Teddies...preferably the girls 'special ones'. Luckily she doesn't destroy them; she just likes to collect them.

What is your favorite memory?

That's a tricky one since there have been so many funny times. Seeing her bounce around on the trampoline with the girls, trying to fill the paddling pool as she steals the hose, hide and seek in the long grass with the children as a puppy; you can also guarantee that if there is a

pond at a posh family BBQ she will find it (over and over again).

If you could change one thing what would it be?

She does tend to pull on her lead. But we are working on it and making progress.

If Luna was a person what would her job be?

Nursery Nurse because she is so patient and gentle with children especially Ellie who was petrified with dogs before Luna came along.

What silly pet name do you have for her?

Lunnie toons

What is her favourite treat?

A nice BIG bone

Who is her best friend?

A Malamute/German Shepherd called Nala

What is the naughtiest thing she has ever done?

Jumped the 4ft fence at the top of our garden, getting out onto the football fields and taking us an hour to catch her again. We now have a 7ft fence in place!

Where is her favorite walk?

She loves Dunwich forest but also Walberswick beach is one of our regular walks...basically anywhere with water!

Printed in Great Britain
by Amazon